China Miéville is the author of various works of fiction and non-fiction. His novels include *The City & The City*, *Embassytown* and his latest book, *Railsea*. His non-fiction includes *Between Equal Rights*, a study of international law. He is three-times winner of the Arthur C. Clarke Award, and has also won the Hugo, World Fantasy and British Science Fiction awards. He lives and works in London. chinamieville.net

ISBN 978-1908906-14-4
eISBN 978-1908906-15-1

Published in the United Kingdom in 2012 by The Westbourne Press
1

A shorter version of this essay was first published in *The New York Times Magazine* in March 2012. This full text is available at londonsoverthrow.org

Printed and bound by CPI Anthony Rowe, Chippenham, SN14 6LH

The Westbourne Press
26 Westbourne Grove, London W2 5RH
www.westbournepress.co.uk

London's Overthrow

China Miéville

The Westbourne Press

London's Overthrow

November – December 2011

SHOVE YOUR HANDS in your pockets and set out. In London in winter it's nearly pitch at half-past-four. By six, you're in the night city, and in backstreets you can be alone for a long time.

Some chance conjunction of latitude and climate: in this city artificial light cuts darkness like nowhere else. There are no trees like these, streetlit up, fractal cutouts. When you were a kid you ran through this bluster and raindrops so tiny they were like dust falling in all directions, not just down, and missed it even while you were in it.

There's been a revolution in remembrance. Digital photography's democratised the night-shoot. One touch at the end of a sleepy phone call on your way home, you can freeze the halo from streetlamps, the occluded moon, night buses, cocoons shaking through brick cuts, past all-night shops. Right there in your pocket, a lit-up memory of now.

THIS IS AN era of CGI end-times porn, but London's destructions, dreamed-up and real, started a long time ago. It's been drowned, ruined by war, overgrown, burned up, split in two, filled with hungry dead. Endlessly emptied.

In the Regency lines of Pimlico is Victorian apocalypse. Where a great prison once was, Tate Britain shows vast, awesome vulgarities, the infernoward-tumbling cities of John Martin, hybrid visionary and spiv. But tucked amid his kitsch nineteenth-century brilliance are stranger imaginings. His older brother Jonathan's dissident visions were unmediated by John's showmanship or formal expertise. In 1829, obeying the Godly edict he could hear clearly, Jonathan set York Minster alight and watched it burn. From Bedlam – he did not hang – he saw out his life drawing work after astonishing work of warning and catastrophe. His greatest is here.

Another diagnostic snapshot.

London's Overthrow. Scrappy, chaotic, inexpert, astounding. Pen-and-ink scrawl of the city shattered under a fusillade from heaven, rampaged through by armies, mobs, strange vengeance. Watching, looming in the burning sky, a lion. It is traumatised and hurt.

The lion is an Emblem too
that England stands but on one Foot

With the urgency of the touched, Martin explains his own metaphors.

and that has lost one Toe
Therefore long it cannot stand

The lion looks out from its apocalypse at the scrag-end of 2011. London, buffeted by economic catastrophe, vastly reconfigured by a sporting jamboree of militarised corporate banality, jostling with social unrest, still reeling from riots. Apocalypse is less a cliché than a truism. This place is pre-something.

30 NOVEMBER. ABOVE the invisible bridge at Blackfriars, red Victorian pilings jutting from the Thames, helicopters dangle like ugly Christmas baubles. They surveil thronging streets. Two million public-sector workers strike today, and tens of thousands of them and their supporters are whooping through central London.

Mary Ezekiel, lifelong Londoner, Highgate by way of Hackney, staff nurse at University

College London Hospital, itemises the effects pension cuts, the action's cause, will have. She flattens down her red t-shirt. Much British tat is emblazoned with the cloying World War II propaganda slogan 'Keep Calm and Carry On'. 'Get Angry', Ezekiel's shirt demands instead, 'and Fight Back'. 'All the speakers have been amazing', she says. 'That's what I feel positive about. I just hope it reaches *Mr Cameron*' – she says the Prime Minister's name disdainfully – 'in his *mansion*.'

Cameron first denounced, then dismissed the day's action. For the Right, strikes are both devilish and pathetic, have both terrible and absolutely no effects.

'The perils of marching!' a young woman laughs, pushing banners out of her face. 'Lashed by flags!' A thousands-strong sprawl of bobbing cloth and cardboard. The logo of the Society of Radiographers wobbles near placards of the Worker-Communist Party of Iran. Holding up a huge pink triangle, a young Ugandan man, Abbey, says, 'We are helping gay asylum seekers from all over the world, especially Uganda, Nigeria, Cameroon, Senegal.' He's there to support the workers. It's all linked, he explains. Cuts to social spending, soaring tuition fees, scapegoating.

Another animal watches from above, like the lion, but this one with relish. Sabbas waves an extraordinary papier-mâché dog head. 'It's the riot dog,' he says. 'Or the riot dogs, because there's more than one riot dog over there.'

London homage to Athenian animal rebellion. Loukanikos, Kanellos and Louk. Unfazed by tear gas, canine presences at every demonstration against the austerity demanded by those who do not need to be austere. Matter-of-factly, Sabbas translates the dog's slogan, its injunction to rulers: '"Cut your own throat".'

NOT IN THE manner Jonathan Martin predicted, but the church and its priests – 'blind Hipacrits, Saarpents and Vipears' – have been shoved abruptly front and centre of crisis. 15 October: Occupy LSX, one of the world's proliferating hashtag movements, converges on the financial district that declares itself, in synecdochic presumption, the City of London. Its participants are aiming for Paternoster Square, the stock exchange, to protest those who brought us to this trembling. Entrance, though, is not a right: the square, like great and growing swathes of corporatised London, once public, these days only pretends to be, and that if you ask nicely. Police block entrance. The protestors set up outside, by a convenient next-door cathedral. St Paul's, Christopher Wren's post-Great Fire masterpiece. A grassroots response to one cataclysm in the splendid shadow of another to another.

Christ's authorities dither. In *London's Overthrow*, they hold their bibles the wrong way round: in London 2011, they start legal action. Two priests resign from the Cathedral hierarchy. More priestly dithering. The Cathedral closes, muttering about safety. The protestors protest that. Ditheration. St Paul's opens again. The

Archbishop of Canterbury offers careful hedged sympathy for the protestors' concerns. Litigation is left up to the City of London Corporation, the unique, rich, secretive local authority.

So here is the structure of Occupy Everywhere, by Cheapside, Milton's birthplace, now an anodyne corporate high street, near Cornhill and Threadneedle Street, hubs of finance. Suited women and men pass the tea tent, the tent university with its whiteboard program of talks, the tent library. Some pause to read the patchwork of signs and cuttings fixed on the canvas and on the pillars of local shops. The Revolution will not be Branded. Don't Attack Iran. Stop Protecting Bondholders, Let Banks Fail.

An expensively dressed man in his mid-50s blinks and, with immaculate posh politeness, declines a request for an on-record opinion of his new neighbours. He goes back to reading the walls. Financial Justice is a Gospel Imperative.

ADS FIND PLACES to root that aren't even places. They sprout on the backs of travelcards, the surfaces of the ticket machines that sell them. The fronts of every step out of the Tube, so, rising from the earth, you're faced with strips of meaningless enthusiasm for product. 'All about me the red weed clambered among the ruins'. Marketing chokes London as vigorously as

Wells' end-of-the-world Martian flora. Outside Waterloo station, at a bus stop, LoveFilm projects an endless loop of bait-drivel onto a building across the road, so its visions lurch into an-amorphic frights on the sides of every bus that passes. And this commercial has a soundtrack. Now, close your eyes, you still can't opt out.

THE GOSPEL IMPERATIVE is broken.

The pay gap between the highest and lowest paid in the UK has grown faster than in any other developed country, spiking since 2005. In 2008, average income of the top 10 per cent was twelve times that of the lowest. Their riches wax.

We others are told to tighten belts. Tax rates for the wealthiest have dropped, even as the gap between the merely rich and the utterly wealthy has grown.

One of capitalism's defences is the outrage-fatigue it engenders.

We're approaching Victorian levels of inequality, and London's more unequal than anywhere else in the country. Here, the richest 10 per cent hold two-thirds of all wealth, the poorest *half*, one-twentieth. A fifth of working residents in the London boroughs of Brent, Newham, Waltham Forest, Barking and Dagenham earn less than a living wage. Unemployment in the city is above 400,000, and rising. Almost a quarter of young Londoners are out of work. A wrenching 40 per cent of London children live in poverty.

The numbers mean death. Travel the grey Jubilee line. Eight stops, east from Westminster to Canning Town. Each stop, local life expectancy goes down a year.

From where you've got out, over the river you can see the dome, blister-memento of London's pathetic millennium.

2011. Stagnation and money cataclysm. Boardroom pay goes up 50 per cent. Still, in London, defenders of privilege aren't quite so prone to open swagger as their US counterparts. Yes, magazines like *Hello* and *Heat*, programs like *Made in Chelsea*, celebrate conspicuous consumption by celebrities and local gilded youth. Yes, the *Financial Times' How To Spend It* supplement, a guide to luxury and chic commodities, is enough to make a placid liberal nostalgic for the guillotine.

But the propaganda never fully took. 1998: Lord Mandelson, New Labour grandee, declares that Labour – that traditionally working-class party –

is 'intensely relaxed about people getting filthy rich'. People, though, refuse to forget that the filthy riches of the filthy rich are not unrelated to the filthy poverty of others. The declaration remained infamous.

Arguments for swollen pay packets among London's 1 per cent and their apparatchiks tend to have a semi-apologetic, semi-sulky ring: it's necessity, the global market, the like-it-or-not real world. Not, as might be more common on Wall Street, moral right. Ineluctibility as self-justification: its fans cite the City of London's strength, its riches, as reason not to target its riches, its strength.

We slump under sado-monetarism. There are other ways. For years Alan Freeman was an economist with the Greater London Authority, working with both mayors. He leans forward in his chair, explaining what's wrong with London's still-massive economy, and how to fix it. He bullet points. 'Build two million homes ... edufare in the place of workfare ... invest in innovation. Quintuple government funding of R&D, extend R&D to the arts ... put growth back and (it's easy to show) the tax coffers will overflow.'

Statues of dragons punctuate the streets of the City, symbols of the area. Less Beasts of Revelation than priggish, arch draconine bureaucrats, more tetchy than rampant. But they guard gold like Smaug.

CHRISTMAS TIME IN London, lights in all areas. Celebrities, minor to middling, gurn out from posters for pantomimes.

The ultrarich might stick to Chelsea and Belgravia, the wealthy stay out of North Woolwich, but in Stoke Newington, in Kensal Rise rich and poor are up close. Islington, north London, a shorthand, these days, for smug affluence, is also the fifth most deprived borough in the capital, with the second highest child-poverty rate in England, a crime rate double the national average. This is London.

The high street's in trouble in this economy. Too, Londoners are anxious about a loss of particularity. A tide of commercial entropy tugs shopping precincts towards indistinguishability, pedestrian brandscapes. The city resists somewhat, especially that zone between suburbs and centre, not quite yet worth the big logo beasts' hungriest attentions. Areas like Balham and Brent, the defining stretches of London, unkempt and irresistible. Here are still the distinct decors of plenty of local shops. Pound stores, crammed cornucopias of bits and pieces and household goods, put their discounted bars of soap and most colourful clothes baskets outside, brooms and mopheads like bunting.

The cheap laundrettes that serve these areas could be portals. The secret of teleportation. Go in past identical 70s-style signs for service washes, in Newham in the east, in Haringey to the north, Lambeth and Lewisham, through the smell of dryers, you enter shared laundretteness, as if you might exit a completely other establishment, in Waltham Forest, Dagenham, Kilburn.

So come out in Kilburn High Road. Here like the street itself, Christmas lights are amiable, vivid and tatty. Shooting stars, little tannenbaums, presents in all colours. It's similar in Neasden up the road, in Brixton and Stockwell down south. Bunting, robot Santas ho-ho-ho-ing, lines of business, broken with dead shops, furred with tinsel. There are ghoulshops, of course, here where the unrich live, pawnbrokers and 'money shops' for short-term loans.

Businesses are closing uptown too, but on the King's Road and Knightsbridge, tchotchkes still go for comedically high prices. The only austerity here is aesthetic. The beasts of Bond Street are bird-footed silver egg-cups from Aspreys, fox and hart masks on mannequins unbothered by lights much sleeker and fewer in colour than those in the Kilburn windows.

You can do class analysis of London with Christmas lights. Glance in the gloaming of late Dec-

ember through the front windows of houses. In estates and cheaper dwellings, the season's celebrated with chromatic surplus. Get smarter, the middle-class occupants strive to distinguish themselves with white-lit Christmas trees.

Ah, good taste, as Picasso may or may not have said, what a dreadful thing. It's preposterous, this doomed attempt to dekitsch Christmas. Delight inheres in the too-muchness. But class markers have long been excessively important to the English culturati. Now in December, white lights and silver ornaments are seasonal peacock tails, with bleached feathers.

IN 2010, THE Labour Party was pushed out of government, and the Conservatives joined forces with the Liberal Democrats to take power. The conventional, if misleading, transatlantic analogy is that of Labour to the Democrats and the Conservatives to the Republicans. What, then, is the Liberal Democrat Party?

A mooncalf formulation. Fag-end descendent of Whigs, anti-trade-union social democrats, free-traders, social liberals, beachcombing disparate inspirations. The rightward lurch of the Labour Party under Blair allowed the LibDems to accrete a certain sheen. Which tarnished at astounding rate when they became part of the ConDem government – such a pitch-perfect portmanteau – signing up to and off on a Thatcherite agenda, privatisation in the health service, cutting the Education Maintenance Allowance that helped lower-income school students, undermining comprehensive education in state schools by pushing selection, the siphoning off of preferred pupils, creating a zero-sum game among proliferating local schools, attacking any nominal agenda of universalism. Melissa Benn, educationalist, calls the model 'rigid centralisation with widespread privatisation'. They tore up a promise not to increase university tuition fees. That last in particular helped radicalise a wave of students whose protests in 2010 started the backlash that, with fits and starts, continues.

Today the default demeanour of the LibDem politician is chippy defensiveness, plus/minus shame. Their left wing performs its lachrymosity and discomfort, their rugged pro-marketeers – like Deputy Prime Minister and party leader Nick Clegg – mutter about hard choices. Betrayal as machismo. Once a *soi-disant* progressive alternative, now they are Tory-enablers.

The economy toilets. Prices rise during a hecatomb of services. Libraries are closing. Social services are slashed. 'What else', laments the front page of the *Kilburn Times*, 'is left for them to cut?'

There's strife beyond the public sector. Several days after the strike, electricians working for the construction company Balfour Beatty walk out in protest against aggressive new contracts. People are fighting to stand still, whatever line of work they're in.

'There are clients that maybe I don't particularly like the sound of ... really bossy and pushy,' Sabina says. 'Now I'd be more likely to consider clients like that.' Sabina has been a sex worker in the capital for twenty years. 'What's happened in the last, maybe, four or five years is ... that more women are going into prostitution, and also women who left are going back, because they find it hard to make ends meet ... what are our options? How are we supposed to survive?'

Some troubles are unique, of course, and very serious, for women in this sector. 'I know two women who've been raided, lost their places and are now working outdoors ... that's a lot more dangerous ... it's absolutely the last resort. But the raids and the whole kind of crackdown on prostitution are driving women to work on their own.'

Other troubles of these parlous times are more familiar. 'Petrol costs have gone up. Parking in London is horrendous.' A universal jeremiad. 'We sex workers are just like everybody else.' Sabina speaks with the patience of someone who has explained this many times before. 'You know, we're trying to keep ourselves and our families together.'

29 NOVEMBER. STRATFORD, East London, is being reconfigured on a biblical scale, like a Martin doom. From the acres of mud and blue wrappings of the Olympic Park juts the city's new monument, the ArcelorMittal Orbit, by the artists Anish Kapoor and Cecil Balmond, a vast sculpture of knotting girders like a snarled Gaian hernia. Its name is a corporate grandiosity on the part of its donor, the richest man in Britain. Near it is the stadium, its post-Olympic future a question mark, with bickerings and legal shenanigans ongoing. There's Zaha Hadid's aquatic centre, its celebrated lines ruined by temporary seating.

At the southern end of the development site, the walkway is on the path of an old sewer. Oh London, you drama queen. You didn't have to do that. We watch from the route of effluent.

Author Iain Sinclair has written this walk before. He's an old hand at this scholarly, sceptical tour. He watches the city change shape from under an unlikely baseball cap, with polite dislike.

The Olympics are slated to cost taxpayers £9.3bn. In this time of 'austerity', youth clubs and libraries are expendable fripperies; this expenditure, though, is not negotiable. The uprisen young of London, participants in extraordinary riots that shook the country last summer, do the maths. 'Because you want to host the Olympics, yeah,' one participant told researchers, 'so your country can look better and be there, we should suffer'.

This is a city where buoyed-up audiences yell advice to young boxers in Bethnal Green's York Hall, where tidal crowds of football fans commune in scabrous chants, where fans adopt local heroes to receive those Olympic cheers. It's not sport that troubles those troubled by the city's priorities.

Mike Marqusee, writer and activist, has been an East London local and a sports fan for decades. American by birth, he nonetheless not only understands and loves cricket, of all things, but even wrote a book about it. He's excited to see the athletics when they arrive up the road from him in July. Still, he was, and remains, opposed to the coming of the Olympics. 'For the reasons that've all been confirmed. These mega-events in general are bad for the communities where they take place, they do not provide long-term employment, they are very exploitative of the area in which they take place. The priorities become the development for the games.'

On the 'Greenway', Sinclair mourns the lost. The unplanned London. Allotments; scrub; pokey businesses and local houses. Stratford animals, with the edgeland in which they thrived. 'I love that.' He gestures at a construction sign, reads its claim sardonically. '"Improving the image of construction." Improving the image of *de*struction.'

We're shunted on a sight-seeing route, down pedestrian runnels. 'You can't go off-piste. Very much not.'

The paths, the enormous structures are neurotically planned and policed. For the area to be other than a charnel ground of Ozymandian skeletons in thirty years, it'll have to develop like a living thing. That means beyond the planners', beyond any, preparations.

The representative of the Olympic Park Legacy Company laughs quietly down the phone at that. 'Yes. You really hit the nail on the head. I'll be honest, it's a constant struggle. Not surprisingly, the planning decisions team who essentially are the arbiters of our planning applications wants comfort and certainty, then you're kind of going, well, the future lies a long way out, and we need to be a little light on our feet. Is it easy? No, you're right, planning is very constrained, and it's a kind of blunt tool to do something where, you want places that are like those grittier, more diverse places'.

Her thoughtful honesty is refreshing. Mostly what we get in London is unending rah-rah from official channels. Two weeks after Sinclair's morose sewage pilgrimage, at the London Policy Conference, a high-powered talking shop for urbanologists, politicians and academics in the brutalist concrete art zone of London's South

Bank Centre, Mayor Boris Johnson chortlingly describes those sceptical of the Games as 'the gloomadon poppers!' Johnson is crush-heckled: someone in the audience bleats that we all love him. The mayor is a ninja of bumptiousness, a man with a genius for working rooms full of the easily pleased. 'The many gloomsters!' he beams, still on Olympic theme.

The Games' security plans grow ever more dystopian and surreal. There will be snipers in helicopters; jets; warships in the Thames; more troops on duty in London than in Afghanistan.

'They won't do it,' Marqusee says, 'but what would have been nice is if they'd made these the austerity games in a nice way. Just get rid of everything else, it's not appropriate, it's just going to be the sports, and we'll enjoy it, everyone'll go half-cost, no big hotels ... and you know, this is London!' He says that with the pleasure of the Londoner by choice. 'No, we're not going to compete with Beijing, we're not that kind of place anyway, we're not an authoritarian state that can get 10,000 people to march up and down. But why not, you know, just be who we are? Get some local kids out to do some hip hop or whatever.'

The Olympic Park recedes. Sinclair leads on toward the Stratford Station with its new soulectomied shopping centre Westfield. Past the Abbey Mills Pumping Station, built deliberately, in strange Victorian homage, to be 'a cathedral of sewage'. At Abbey Creek, at last the coiffed zone ends. A scrubside cloacal sump, a quag of runoff reefed astonishingly with discarded tires and once-sunk supermarket trolleys, revealed by low tide.

Call it apocalypse tourism, but we stare at it a lot longer than we do at the twisted tower.

'I KIND OF see a beauty in all that architecture'. Tottenham, north London, is an area of extraordinary ethnic diversity and local pride, and one troubled by unemployment, poverty, poor housing. In the video for *Unorthodox* by London rapper Wretch 32, filmed in the area's Broadwater Farm Estate – notorious for riots in 1985 – it's startlingly beautiful. 'I kind of want to turn it on its head,' says Ben Newman, the director, of the cliché. 'I know a lot of people film and represent those areas in a negative way.' Instead, the mixed-up area captured in the stairwells is a good, boisterous London dream, and true.

There's another Tottenham, equally true. Jonathan Martin prophesies: 'London shall be all in flames'. It's scribbled below the lion. Who's mad now? There was an image on endless repeat last summer. A conflagration, the charcoal shell of a local landmark, a well-known carpet shop. This was the first of a series of disturbances that spread over successive nights around London and the country. Britons saw loop after loop of images of buildings on fire, smashed glass, streets in raucous refusal. Youths taking TVs, clothes, carpets, food from broken-open shops, sometimes with dizzy exuberance, sometimes with what looked like thoughtful care.

The aftermath is panicked reaction. Courts became runnels for judicial cruelty, sentences twice, three times anything usual for similar crimes. The government's watchdog announces that police might use live ammunition against those setting fires – some were teenagers – in future.

14 December. In an effort to make sense of the extraordinary events, the *Guardian* newspaper and the London School of Economics release 'Reading the Riots', a joint report on what happened. What they have discovered, through extensive research and interviews, is that what motivated many of those on the streets was resentment of police, and a deep sense of injustice.

Eyes roll with the duh.

Self-evident or not, this does not convince everyone. Theresa May, the Conservative Home Secretary, blames instead 'sheer criminality'. It's singalong for the Right. They know this tune: it was played after the Brixton riots of 1981 and 1985, Tottenham 1985, after every riot in London, or anywhere, since forever. While May's denunciation and denial of the obvious continues, her own department quietly gets on with examining the police's stop-and-search powers, a cause of huge resentment among young Londoners, which – when do such powers not? – disproportionately affect minorities.

'Feeling powerless, for me, is a very dangerous thing, that we've seen in the riots,' says Symeon Brown at the London Policy Conference. Brown's a young man from Tottenham himself, a youth activist, a researcher who worked on the *Guardian* report. During the disturbances, he explains, giving himself the voice of one of those involved, came 'that sense that for once in my life I had power'.

The words echo astonishingly across years, one riot to another. Dambudzo Marechera, Zimbabwean *poete maudit*, wrote 'Smash, Grab, Run' about his experiences in Brixton in the 1980s.

And just this once in my black British life
Exploded the atoms in me into atoms of power

There is a key and concrete factor not mentioned at the conference. A name is missing, a name that recurs in interviews with the riots' participants, in tweets from the upsurging streets themselves.

Mark Duggan. The young man shot dead by the Metropolitan Police on 4 August 2011.

'We've been saying in meetings ever since the beginning of this year that there was a ... powerful change of anger out there in the community. It wasn't difficult to pick it up, you could just go to public meetings.' Helen Shaw is co-director of Inquest, an organisation dedicated to the investigation of contentious deaths in official custody. She sounds like someone sad to be right. 'So I suppose the surprise is the police claiming they didn't have a sense of how angry people were.'

Mark Duggan's family were denied information. Misinformation about their dead son was leaked. 6 August. A demonstration supporting the family outside Tottenham Police Station. The key moment that occurred when the police intervene, which many who were present say was the spark for everything that followed, is immortalised on YouTube. Its rage-capitalled title is its own misspelt explanation: '16 YEAROLD GIRL ATTACKED BY TOTTENHAM RIOT POLICE WHICH STARTED THE RIOTS!'

In Britain between 1998 and 2009, there were at least 333 deaths in police custody, eighty-seven of them after restraint by officers. Not a single officer has ever been convicted for a single one. Of all the more and less unsubtle ways young Londoners – those not Made In Chelsea, those not rich – are told that they are not terribly important, none are so overt or cruel as this.

Sitting so straight on a raised dais, in so immaculate a uniform, that he looks like a ventriloquist's dummy, the Metropolitan Police's new commissioner, Bernard Hogan-Howe, tells the conference in an avuncular voice nothing about Mark Duggan's death. He talks, rather, enthusiastically if nebulously, about his plan for 'Total Policing'. He enthuses about large forces zooming into small areas and clamping down on minor infractions. He mentions uninsured vehicles.

Helen Shaw has a different understanding. She suspects Total Policing will mean 'a much more aggressive police presence, a stance that's more aggressive, and more about fear'. Indeed, Hogan-Howe says he wants 'to put fear into the hearts of criminals'. Shaw is more stark. 'We think we'll see more deaths.'

Constituencies not traditionally antipathetic to the police have been shocked by its fervent enthusiasm for 'kettling', corralling demonstrators tightly without charge, food, water or release, for hours. Officer Mark Kennedy is exposed as a mole among non-violent ecological activists, becomes emblematic of an extraordinary and illegal campaign of infiltration and sexual deceit. The brutal policing of student protests on 9 December 2010 left one young man, Alfie Meadows, in hospital with brain injuries. At that same protest, police hauled Jody McIntyre, a twenty-year-old with cerebral palsy, from his wheelchair, dragging him across the ground. At a demonstration on 1 April 2009, an unresisting and uninvolved newspaper seller, Ian Tomlinson, was hit by the police and died shortly after. And there is Mark Duggan, about whom each rumour initially leaked – that he shot first, that he shot at all – is proved one by one to be untrue.

The attacks on McIntyre and Tomlinson were watched, recorded, by the gaze of cellphone cameras. Collecting notes from a troubled culture. Police seem still not quite to grasp that these little machines preserve more than nocturnal melancholy.

THE RIOTS HAD a soundtrack.

In 1995, insolently young south Londoners Eddie Otchere and Andrew Green, as James T. Kirk and Two Fingers, published *Junglist*, a brilliant neglected text of London gnosis, backstreet Modernism, a strange riff on being young in the city and in thrall to the dance music of the time. Jungle, deep structured by beats, full of industrial blarings like the mating calls of old factories. London music conducted by aliens.

Sixteen years, generations and crossbreeds later, two descendant musics tussle for hegemony – dubstep and grime. The former is all wobbling bass, looped fuzzed samples, tight drums. It's viralled fast into commercial cliché and star turns, uninteresting but for a few left-field experimenters, like the 'post-dubstep' melancholy of London genius Burial. Tracks for those nightwalks.

Grime is the bratty, bolshy sibling. The riot music. Born out of London's pirate radio scene, shouty vocals over frenetic beats. Indelibly London, saturated with the localism of the city itself. In grime, representing your area, sometimes down to your street, is key. Not overtly political music, for the most part, it is, though, to the horror of splenetic politicians, an angry one.

30 November. Shoreditch. We're south of the White Cube gallery, in old streets embedded in folk song. Working-class once, now arts-gentrified, wedged full of subtle-fonted bar-signs, boutiques and hangouts. Downstairs at the club East Village, it's the launch of Rival's EP, *Lord Rivz*.

The music goes like an adrenalised heart. All the movements in the thundering dark hall, dancing, nodding, twitching in place, are stiff-limbed. Tune segues into tune that flaunts its discordance, its jerking rhythm: it's ornery, a kind of anti-dance music, demanding you move but making you work to work it. There's no aggro, not among the dancers, despite all the screwfaces, wincing like they hurt, making some noise when they hear classic tracks. And then the MCs step up, and there's a surge for the decks. 'Music,' Dan Hancox shouts, 'to storm the Treasury to.'

That's the kind of joke can get a person closed down. Hancox is a writer on politics, on grime, on youth. We're buffeted by what they called the soundtrack to the riots. Music of this austerity moment.

It's exhausting, being smacked around by east

London beats. We break from the club, stand outside near the smokers and enjoy the cold air. Hancox's excitement ebbs. 'It dampens the spirits a bit,' he says. 'It's about a third full?'

About a third, yes. There's been a sustained campaign against grime from all establishment sides. Hancox mutters about form 696. The Met uses this notorious risk-assessment paperwork in deciding to allow – or not to allow – musical events. Until 2008, almost unbelievably, its original wording ferreted ingenuously, 'Is there a particular ethnic group attending? If "yes" please state group.'

Outrage. The wording changed, the targeting remained.

It was hard for Hancox to track down a night to go to at all.

THE GRIME CREWS are right; each part has its own specificity. It wouldn't be the worst sin to call it 'soul'. Camden nostalgic for itself, giant nipple rings and boots on its shops like discards from a punk god. Chelsea riverside. Drab towerblocks in Silvertown by the sugar factory. Façades echo Deco, variably magnificent: Kilburn's Gaumont State; the Hoover building in Perivale; East Finchley Tube. There are skateparks under the concrete sky of the Westway and the big sky of south London: 'Brixton Beach', those graffitied concrete dunes. Each is irreducible, each a gallimaufry, and each clines into its neighbour zones. Topography patchworks – seventeenth-century noses up through building-years to horrible modern brick the colour of mustard, 80s, 90s and noughties jostling with the centuries-old stones.

Someone's left a sofa under a hoarding at Dudden Hill, overlooking the railway cut. You could spectate the city. Keep your phone out, and not to talk. London's preening.

15 DECEMBER. TWO boys get on a 98 bus, heading from northwest London to the centre. They swagger upstairs, lounge on the front seats, turn their phones into inadequate speakers and drawl along. 'Every Saturday Rap Attack, Mr

Magic, Marley Marl, I let my tape rock 'til my tape popped'. Like they know what tape is.

You want to see how much London hates its young – some of them: 'Let's be honest,' says the writer Owen Jones, 'they're not talking about Etonians' – watch them play music on public transport. Everyday silliness, adolescent thoughtlessness are treated like social collapse. Of which there's a fair bit going around, true, but does it really inhere in this?

'On the one hand you have this patronising attitude towards young people, coddling them and everything,' says Saleha Ali, twenty-five, volunteer coordinator at WORLDwrite, an education charity in Hackney. 'And on the other hand you have heavy-handed regulation, so there's a hysteria about young people getting really drunk, going out, and all these kinds of things, it's just like panic, oh my God, what are we creating, a generation of monsters?'

Quotidian teen truculence is as suspect as violence. Which does happen too, of course.

The night Hackney rioted, there were images local resident, journalist and photographer transplanted from Paris, Valeria Costa-Kostritsky, had to record. She was out, like hundreds of others, among her neighbours. And it was all fine until a young man reached like an older brother around her neck, took her camera by the strap, punched the slight young woman repeatedly and hard in the face when she tried to stop him.

'Immediately, on that day, you see lots of people on Facebook saying horrible things about the rioters. Mostly saying "scum".' Certainly, being so savagely attacked, she remembers, 'gave me an insight into how uncool violence is, how scary it is'. She laughs, self-deprecating about her assault-satori. 'But it would never occur to me to, because of that, to call a group of people scum. To me that's crossing a line. Something I don't do. People are people.' Her disgust is audible. 'Even if they do something, you know, not nice to you, they are people.'

Tinny music on a bus raises disproportionate ire. Travellers shift and glare as fourteen-year-olds give themselves soundtracks, like they're boxers. Not all, but a fair few of the older passengers look wrathful.

Who cares? You're getting off in five minutes, he's fourteen and trying it on a bit and boisterous to fill the city with music.

In 1998, Tony Blair ushered into being ASBOs, Antisocial Behaviour Orders. Sharp laws, the better for society, like Cronus, like a traumatised hamster, to eat its children. These startling civil orders criminalise legal behaviour, individually, tailor-making offences. A seventeen-year-old is banned from swearing. Another told he could go to jail if he drops his trousers. A nineteen-year-old barred by law from playing football in the street.

'I do think there is something very particular about here.' Camila Batmanghelidjh, the founder of Kids Company, one of the best-known figures in British child welfare. She leans her head on her hand, arranges her trademark, flowing, vivid clothes. 'I have a hunch. Which is that the British are very ashamed of vulnerability. So what happens is whereas another culture might look back on their childhood and say "God, I was so cute, I thought clouds were cotton wool", the British will look back and say "God, I was so stupid, I thought clouds were cotton wool".'

Catastrophe generates the beasts it needs. In London, in the UK, the term 'feral youth' is absolutely routine. Media and politicians deploy it without much controversy. As if such a spiteful, shocking, bestialising phrase does not disgrace every mouth from which it spills. Its utterance is not a diagnosis, but a symptom.

28 NOVEMBER. OF London's dead landscapes, there are few like the Heygate Estate, ruin on a Martin scale. A dizzying sprawl of concrete in Southwark, a raised town, great corridored blocks, walkways over communal gardens. Slabs of buildingness. It's all but empty. It's to be demolished. Even were it not stuffed with asbestos, that would take a long time.

Laura Oldfield Ford leads the way. Don't call her a psychogeographer. Many do, and she abjures it. The term's travelled a long way from its origins as a radical French research program to reconfigure urban space. It cross-fertilised with the tradition of London visionary writing, tangled up with urban invocation. Now it's a local cliché. A lazy label for hip decay tourism.

Ford, not twee, frequents wreckage. An excoriating critic of neoliberalism and its banalisation of space, she reconfigures her long London walks into raging, celebrated post-punk art. 'I wanted to take the term psychogeography but I wanted it to be about the radicalism of it, not this kind of ... leylines and all that,' she withers. Past the graves of shops, the long, long-shuttered front of what was once The Institute of Traditional Karate-Do and Performing Arts. You could follow her with your eyes closed, so loud are her steps.

Through lagoons of drifting late autumn leaves in the shadow of the Heygate enormities. In a very few places is proof of life. A nicknack and net curtains in a window, a car below. Someone's maintaining a small vegetable garden. There's graffiti, but not so much as you might think.

In a clearing between benches and the remains of a playground, young men conclave. It's startling to see anyone after so long alone. It's an affront not to have the whole world to ourselves. But then they set off. In ragged line. They accelerate, vaulting, along walls, bouncing one by one from brick detail to concrete outcrop, up onto low roofs, over and under flaking painted barriers, watched by pigeons.

They're training in *parkour*, another French import. Psychogeography of the limbs, filtered through Kung-Fu movies. No number of ads, music videos, station idents featuring roof-bounding like this can make it boring, can alter the fact that watching the *parkouristes* lurch in ways architects never intended along the buildings' innards is quite beautiful. There's salvage. A tough ruin ballet.

IT'S A WONDER it was so easy to get inside. Buildings of London are jagged for protection, their defences as various as any animal adaptations. Archaeologies of wire. It's the relict ancestor of razorwire that proliferates, brambles made of rust, on backstreet lock-ups. Walltops from Greenwich to Wembley, Ealing to Walthamstow are dorsal ridges of shards in old cement – bottleglass, crockery, bust-up mirror. Seven years misfortunes weaponised against intrusion. They sprout like werewolf hair. As if, in defence of property, the city sloughs off brick and is a beast beneath. A rare apocalypse, among London's many.

In South Kensington, the bricks of the Natural History Museum are already animaled, in profusion. Big-headed fish coil around Thames-side lamp-posts. In Hackney are benches with iron camel side-slats. Inaccurate dinosaurs guard one end of Crystal Palace park, sphinxes the other. The lions of Trafalgar Square are sedate, with whole feet. They're in denial.

The Horniman Museum, Forest Hill. Amid its anthropological la-las, its live fish, its art, is a chamber of questionable taxidermy in eccentric taxonomy. Dingy things. Half-bat skeletons flying out of their own skins. A cabinet of dog heads, a starburst of skulls and morose faces. In the centre, point zero of the canine explosion, is a tatty wolf. Its expression has no name. It stares out, its face as horrified as Martin's lion, as angry as the riot dogs of Greece.

IT USED TO be startling to see a fox in London – impossible not to feel the city had slipped into a fable. Now you spot them on any late-night jog. They make their eerie noise and stink up London with musk. In 2011, one of these agents of animal chaos infiltrated the Shard – 32 London Bridge, the city's unfinished tallest building – and climbed a thousand feet above the streets to live on builder's scraps.

At dusk and dawn, green bolts shoot low as flocks of parakeets – 'feral' here no insult – set about bird business. Walking at dawn in the mud of Wormwood Scrubs common, by the prison of the same name, we approach a screaming copse. Incredible flocks of these nonnatives preen and screechingly bicker, overlooking the glow of waking London, the shafts of Hammersmith Hospital.

David Lindo is the Urban Birder, a writer and broadcaster, well-known in the British bird world. To him, these parakeets are bullies, worse than a distraction. He eyes them with dislike.

'See these are black-headed gulls,' he says, looking in another direction. 'Actually that one's a common gull. The common gull,' he says, 'is not common at all.'

A young lesser black-backed gull. A female blackbird. A magpie. Lindo reminisces about the waxwings brought in by last year's snow. But he is indulgent of the non-specialist's fascination with the unlikely parakeets. We wait. They fly in waves, low, hook-billed, hungry into the dawn, and he leads the way into the unbirded trees.

Guano devastation. Limey spatters ruin the winter vegetation like the aftermath of some epochal paintball war.

'They nest in holes,' Lindo says. 'There's anecdotal evidence that they oust our native hole-nesters, like starlings, stock doves and nuthatches. And' – he pauses grimly – 'there's a shortage of holes in Britain as it is.'

FOR ALL OF US. Everyone knows there's a catastrophe, that few can afford to live in their own city. It was not always so.

'The big difference from the American system is that in Britain what we call council housing is publicly owned and provides general-need housing.' Eileen Short is chair of Defend Council Housing. 'It's not welfare housing, it's housing as a right, and this was the model that was used to clear the slums and provide the housing in the crisis years after the First and the Second World Wars, so that across London ... good quality spacious housing of its day was built, which now means that lower-paid and average-paid workers and the elderly and parents and so on can live in some of the most expensive areas of London.' All those streets with both many-coloured Christmas lights and white. 'In Britain even thirty years ago, 30 per cent of the population lived in council housing. And it has a proud and treasured part to play in life for ordinary people.'

But that stock has been depleted for years. Houses taken from the pool were left unreplaced, at rates accelerating fast under Thatcher's right-to-buy schemes from the 1980s. New Labour did nothing to reverse this. The shortage is severe. Rents are rocketing, house prices, stagnating gently or not, are utterly prohibitive. Everyone knows this. Now the government is capping housing benefits, and the Chartered Institute of Housing warns that 800,000 households across the country are likely to be priced out of their own communities as a result. Rough sleeping is up.

The trends are obvious, the results predictable. 'What we think is likely to happen,' says Bharat Mehta, Chief Executive of Trust for London, whose job is to investigate London poverty, 'is that there'll be a movement of people from inner to outer London'.

There is a new turn. This is not neglect. Westminster Council, one of London's richest, moots a 'Civil Contract'. An obligation to the unemployed in its public housing to perform unpaid community work – to call it 'voluntary' in this context would be Orwellian. 'It is a legitimate question,' says Councillor Colin Barrow at the London Policy Conference, 'who will be given the privilege of being able to move into Westminster because they would like to live there at the expense of the taxpayer who has to live in Hornchurch' – a considerably less chichi northeastern suburb. No longer a right, public housing is to be a privilege, policed by gatekeepers.

In Paris, cheap housing is pushed out of sight of the boulevards, to the *banlieues*, the impoverished, underserved, tense suburbs. With its history of public housing, London has always been far more of a medley, incomes jostling together. Now the poor are to be pushed centrifugally, faster and faster. The *banlieue*fication of London is underway.

'WILLESDEN SALVAGE', A sign says. That sounds hopeful. Then: 'We have moved'. November, fog comes down, thick as the fumes above *London's Overthrow*. You realise how little you know the cityscape you love: as the mist evanesces, you don't know what will emerge, if those towers you can suddenly see were there before, or if London grows by congealing smoke.

There is building, just endlessly not of public housing. The city's showcase architecture is elemental. The 30 St Mary Axe building – the

Gherkin – less than a decade old, is established in the skyline. The spine of the Shard soars above London accumulating glass as if it's in solution, growing crystals. Number 20 Fenchurch Street – the Walkie Talkie – rises by now above-ground. It's too early to be sure how such leviathan construction will submit to the city.

Some will be ugly. That might not be the worst sin: that London can metabolise. Centre Point, stubby tower at the junction of Oxford Street and Tottenham Court Road, is ugly, and, if grudgingly, rather loved. But London's growing fake public space abjures the backstreet-and-alleyway gestalt of the city. It and its planners have little room for any urban contingency where railway bridges cut low over streets, on their own business, at angles that make no sense from below, forming strange obliques and acutes with the houses they meet.

The question is whether these new glass boxes of large size can, over time, submit, surrender, become part of the city. This is something that

Canary Wharf, the Docklands financial district begun in the late '80s, every day a thuggish and hideous middle finger flipped glass-and-steel at the poor of the East End, every night a Moloch's urinal dripping sallow light down on the Isle of Dogs, has never done and will never do.

FIND A HOLE, force your parakeet way in. In the City, moments from Bunhill Fields, the dissenters' graveyard where Blake and Bunyan lie, near posh ziggurats of the Barbican estate, is Sun Street. There an empty bank, the UBS building, has been taken over by occupier allies of the St Paul's tent city. They declare it the Bank of Ideas.

'A Public Repossession'. The doorkeepers, serious young counterculturalists, vigorously enforce a no-alcohol policy. You're there for a cabaret, slam poetry in what was once an open-plan workspace.

The officeness of the reconfigured rooms is astonishing. Now they contain sleeping bags, placards, chatty gatherings. Sleeping People! a sign warns on one door. A graffitied figure pokes his head through the false ceiling, passes written comment. Downstairs, children play around their parents as the General Assembly discusses the website. Firefighters politely discuss safety with the new locals.

You ascend an unlit stairwell, very slowly, waiting for the shout, but no one tells you you're not allowed. It's startlingly exhilarating. You're beginning to get it. This is why the psychic economy of squatting, its rejigging of the mind, can end up as important to many squatters as the prosaic financial economy.

Miles south. New Cross. Past a zone of cheap shops and blistered signs, railways and alleyways, a boarded-up backstreet terraced house. You wouldn't think anyone would answer a knock on this.

But inside, Saul's house is warm and lit, it's clean, if a little rough at the edges, there's food in the fridge, the toilet flushes. It vibes like nothing so much as a student flat. Housemates drift in and out. Ali, a gently-spoken Palestinian refugee, stops for tea and chats about his two years in the notorious Harmandsworth detention centre. What is his status now? 'I have no status.'

Saul's hows and whys of squatting. He nods intently and runs through it. He's done it for years.

Find your place – boards on windows and doors a tell – safely gain entry, sort out wires, do the plumbing, smooth relations with locals and landlords.

Squat well. 'It's annoying when people squat badly and it … creates a bad reputation for everyone.'

The why? Property costs at first, of course, but it goes beyond that now. 'Squatting can be seen as just dropping out of mainstream society; avoiding rent, bills, a career, mortgages, responsiblity ... but it can also be understood in its positive aspect.' A culture, a collective. 'As providing or creating space where other types of relationships are possible ... based on trust, sharing, freedom'.

'Sometimes', Saul adds, and he manages to make it seem not forlorn, but good humoured, 'it even happens.'

LONDON'S ACCRETED FROM immigrant generations – Jewish, Caribbean, Bengali, Pakistani, Indian, Chinese, Irish, Polish, Roma, and endlessly on. It is saturated with decades of effort, the grind of antiracist activists remembered in the city's matter: the Claudia Jones Organisation, the CLR James Library. In the built world – the Brick Lane Mosque, previously a synagogue, before that a church – in clothes and music, in London's rapid slang, in the withering of hate-filled chants on football terraces, in attitudes transformed from three, two decades ago, in all the mixed friendships and love affairs, down to its deeps and to Londoners' joy and fortune, London is the most and most successfully multicultural city in Europe.

Diasporas have sustained us. It's a terrible cliché, multiculturalism through food, but there's a reason it's what we reach for. Smart restaurants like St John have rehabilitated English fodder, glorying in pork, blackberries, eulogising offal. Fine. If you're of a certain age and grew up here, you remember that the lucky, rich or recent immigrant families aside, we had no food. We gnawed bread like bleached plastic, cheese like soap. We yowled, a hungry people. New Londoners took pity before the rest of us succumbed to malnutrition and misery, and shared their cuisines. Indian, Jamaican, whatever – name a culinary tradition, it won't be too far to find, near greasy spoons keeping the faith.

Each new group of incomers brings something – now Polish food has mainstreamed, and there's dense bread in the corner shops, *krufki* in supermarkets.

Racism, of course, endures, adapts. According to the exigencies of ideology, casts around for one, then another first-choice hate. Jews in the 1930s, then Black people, then Asians. For the past ten years, Muslims in particular have worn the bulls-eye. If they're women who cover their hair, those few who veil entirely or those who chat into scarf-tucked phones, the hijab hands-free, their choice of headgear is bizarrely troublesome to those whose business it is not. The government's official counterterror strategy includes asking lecturers to report depressed Muslim students. Hate crimes against Muslims rise, fuelled, researchers at the University of Exeter suggest, by the mainstreaming of Islamophobia among politicians and in the media. You can say shocking, scandalous things about Muslims, and opinion-makers do, then push out their chins as if they've been brave.

Feeding on that disgrace, Britain is seeing a mutation of its 'traditional' fascism into a form fixated on these new scapegoats. Emerging from groups like the British National Party and foot-ball hooliganism, the English Defence League aims its spite squarely at Muslims. It follows a familiar trajectory of intimidation: it tries to march in 'Muslim' areas. But it has taken a few unusual turns, too, showing off a (very) few members of colour, Jewish members, gay members. Pitching for a 'liberal' fascism.

But London is London. 'Their situation in London is incredibly weak,' says Martin Smith, a leader of Unite Against Fascism. 'Because London's so integrated,' he adds enthusiastically, 'you can literally go from estate to estate and it's black, white, mums and dads, mixed, all that.'

'I think with migrants,' he continues, pausing slightly, 'you can get what I would call racist sentiments developing, even among Blacks, Asians.' Smith knows this fight. He's optimistic but not relaxed. These are not easy times. The city shakes. 'There could be, I suppose – panic issues could develop around that. I wouldn't rule that out in London. I think it would be hard but I wouldn't rule it out.'

NO WONDER MARTIN'S lion looks haunted. London's full of ghosts – ghostwalks; a city's worth of cemeteries; ghost advertising, scabs of paint on brick. The city invoked something, read a grimoire it shouldn't have. Thatcher's face recurs at every turn, not in clouds of sulfur but of exhaust, on buses bearing posters advertising Meryl Streep's celluloid turn as our erstwhile prime minister. Cabinet reports have been released from the aftermath of other riots across the country, thirty-one years ago. A policy was mooted, they suggest – the point is disputed – of 'managed decline' of the troublesome areas. Leaving them to rot.

Does the repressed return, or never go away?

Lionel Morrison considers the past. Few people are so well poised to parse this present, of press scandals, claim and counterclaim of racism and police misbehaviour, deprivation, urban uprising. A South African radical, facing the death penalty in 1956 for his struggles against apartheid – in his house there is a photograph of him with one of his co-defendants, Nelson Mandela – Morrison got out, came to London in 1960. In 1987, he became the first Black president of the National Union of Journalists. In 2000 he was honoured by the British Government with what is, bleakly amusingly, still called an OBE, Order of the British Empire.

We sit in his home, between English oil portraits that must be two centuries old, and carvings and sculptures from the country of his birth. Is Morrison hopeful? An optimist?

'I've been thinking about it myself,' he says gravely, his voice still strongly accented after all these years. 'In a sense, I'm an optimist. But it hits and completely, constantly kicks at this optimism, you understand?'

The 'it' is everything.

'It's like a big angry wolf having it over here. And it's not prepared to move, and sometimes its legs will go, but slow.' He mimes the animal moving, leaving a little space, a little hole, an exit. 'And people will say, "Ah, we've got it!" And then chop, it goes again.' His hands come down, the wolf's grasp closes.

Outside, north London gets on with its dark. There's an apocalypse more wintery than Martin's conflagration. At the end of all things, Fenris-wolf will eat the sun. Its expression will be of nothing but greed, and it will look out at nothing.

Lionel Morrison doesn't sound despairing. But he does sound tired.

'Every time you do something and nothing goes any further, it eats at you,' he says. 'It starts this *bitterness*.' He says the word slowly. 'And I think this is one of the most terrible things that can take place ... many become hopeless ... it just breaks them down, and they think, "No, I want nothing more to do with this." And then you find others who think, "Well, doing this and nothing happens? Well, let us just wait for things to – for chaos, really, to take place."'

I owe sincere thanks to all who were so generous with their time and help. In addition to those who spoke to me and whose words are quoted in this essay, I am deeply grateful to Neil Arnold, Brenna Bhandar, Mic Cheetham, Rupa DasGupta, Rupert Goold, Maria Headley, Stewart Home, Simon Kavanagh, Victoria Northwood, James Nunn, Dean Robinson, Max Schaefer, Jesse Soodalter, Alberto Toscano, Rukhsana Yasmin, all at the *New York Times* and all at The Westbourne Press.

China Miéville
London, 2012